Grand Harbour about 1957 — **EMPIRE PARKESTON** (1930) with in foreground stern of **EMPIRE GULL** (1945) and in background **EMPIRE ORWELL** (1936)

FERRY MALTA

IL - VAPURI TA GHAWDEX

by Graeme Somner

Published by the World Ship Society
Kendal LA9 7LT
1982

CONTENTS

ISBN O 905617 19 3

HISTORY OF THE FERRY SERVICE BETWEEN MALTA AND GOZO

Half way between Gibraltar (1,141 miles away) and Alexandria (944 miles), lie the Maltese islands of Malta, Gozo and Comino. These islands are the only remaining part of a land bridge connecting Europe (Sicily 58 miles to the North) with the continent of Africa (180 miles to the South), which sank under the Mediterranean Sea some 170,000 years ago. Evidence of Malta's ancient past can be seen in the many caves that exist, relics of the earliest human occupation that have been recovered, and the remains of temples found.

Because of a long line of foreign domination, the Maltese people have gained international character which has enriched their culture. Much of the grandeur is owed to the knights of St John of Jerusalem, who made Malta their home for close on three centuries. Valletta, the capital city, was built by the French Grand Master of the Order, Jean de la Valette, after the epic first siege of the islands in 1565. This city dominates the island's historic harbour, Grand Harbour, the finest natural port in Europe. The total area of the islands is 122 square miles, with Malta being the largest island with a length of 17 miles, and at its widest point 9 miles broad. Gozo is smaller and the corresponding distances are 9 miles and 4½ miles respectively, with Comino even smaller. The coastlines of all the islands are well indented and the population number some 300,000 people, many of whom are engaged in agriculture, especially in Gozo, the most fertile island.

Grand Harbour has for centuries been a haven for ships of many nations, and as trading between nations increased so did the number of vessels calling at Malta. During times of war, Grand Harbour became a naval anchorage and activity was at its peak during the Crimean War (1854-1856), World War I (1914-1918) and in World War II (1939-1945). After the opening of the Suez Canal in 1869, Grand Harbour became a coaling station (and later an oil bunkering station) for the ships moving between Europe and the Far East, and to this facility was added ship repair facilities, an important factor in the island's economy in the last few years, now that the British naval dockyard has been closed down.

Whilst the majority of the inhabitants live on Malta, on which the largest town and only major port is situated, the island of Gozo is less populated being dependant on agriculture rather than providing services. Because of this, there has always been a steady movement of agricultural products to Malta, with locally manufactured and foreign imported goods making up the return traffic to Gozo. Comino is sparsely populated and depends for its supplies on nearby Gozo. There is, therefore, a vital link between Malta and Gozo to be maintained and initially because of the inadequate roads and lack of surface transport (other than by horse), this link was by sea from Grand Harbour to Mgarr Bay, Gozo. A service existed from about 1800, but this was of an irregular nature, maintained by picturesque lateen rigged Gozitan boats, and later schooners. For those faint hearted souls who could not face the sea trip of some 20 miles, the alternative until 1931 was to take horse or carriage up to Marfa, the nearest point on Malta to Gozo — not a popular experience as it took all day — and reaching there, hoisting a lighted straw bale on a mast, when hopefully a fishing boat from Gozo would come over and pick the weary passengers up. This way the sea passage was reduced to something like 4 miles, but the sea conditions of the Comino Channel had still to be suffered even then, and these could be quite severe in winter.

Although steam propelled vessels were in service at Malta from the mid-19th century, it was not until the 1850s that steamers appeared at Gozo, and even then it was only on occasional trips. However, the steamers were more reliable and could more or less be depended upon to complete the journey in a reasonable time, rather than the days that could be experienced by the sailing vessels when adverse winds were met with. The steamers accommodation for passengers was not much better than the sailing vessels, but at least the faster passage time did induce more people to travel to Gozo during holiday and festa times. It is recorded that in August, 1856, the steam tugs SOVEREIGN and DRAGON (1855) made several trips between the islands, and on 19th August, 1859, the steam tugs DRAGON and BULLDOG (1855), together with the steamer SOUTH WESTERN (1858), broke all records by conveying 8,000 passengers to Gozo.

This irregular transport situation continued until 1884, when at the instigation of the Governor of the period, His Excellency Sir John Simmons, and the Bishop of Gozo, Monsignor Pace, the Government invited tenders for the operation of a regular passenger and mail service by steamer between Grand Harbour and Mgarr Bay, where there was a small pier. The service to be provided was on a once-daily basis in winter, and twice in summer, for which a subsidy of £750 per annum would be paid. The Government would deduct the sum of £2 for any trip not operated, except in the case of bad weather, and could also direct the steamer to proceed to Sicily to collect mails coming overland from England, should this be considered necessary. For this latter service, a sum of £25 per round-trip would be paid. The company of O.F. Gollcher & Sons was successful in winning this contract early in 1885, and immediately set about finding a suitable steamer to undertake the sailings. Because the pier at Mgarr Bay was inadequate for steamers to come alongside, passengers and mail would have to be landed by small boat, a state of affairs that continued until 1931.

Gollcher's were fortunate in purchasing the almost new steamer GLENEAGLES of Aberdeen for the sum of £8,000. A Maltese crew took over the 136-foot steamer at Aberdeen on 10th May, 1885, and on the 19th she sailed for Malta, arriving in Grand Harbour on 10th June, 1885. The inaugural sailing to Gozo was made on Saturday, 13th June, when GLENEAGLES with His Excellency The Governor on board sailed from Grand Harbour at 3.0 p.m. She arrived off Mgarr at 4.10 p.m., where she was blessed by the Bishop of Gozo. After the guests were served with a buffet onboard, GLENEAGLES sailed round Gozo and arrived back in Grand Harbour at 9.0 p.m. that night. A twice-daily service was started on the following Monday, with sailings from Grand Harbour at 5.0 a.m. and 3.0 p.m., at a fare of 8 pence single and one shilling return. When the regular steamer started, a levy of one penny per head was collected from the vessel's owners for each passenger landed on Gozo, to pay for a Mass to be said in Mgarr Church for the safe arrival of the passengers. However, as the years passed this custom was dropped although Mass is still said and church bells rung on occasions, but few of the passengers give much thought about their safe arrival these days, being rather more concerned in running to catch their buses!

In October, 1885, proposals were put forward for the need for a breakwater at Mgarr, but action on such a project was still some 45 years away.

As Gollcher's purchased another steamer in 1886, by name LADY DOWNSHIRE, from that time onwards, GLENEAGLES had a relief and on frequent occasions until 1901, LADY DOWNSHIRE took the Gozo crossings when not otherwise engaged on a sailing to Sicily or North Africa. From January, 1892, GLENEAGLES made a regular sailing from Malta to Syracuse once weekly to supplement the sailings made by Italian steamers which carried the mails to and from England overland through Europe. Because of this, until 16th February, 1895, the afternoon sailing on Tuesdays to Gozo, and the Wednesday morning sailings from Gozo were withdrawn to allow GLENEAGLES to undertake the Sicily sailing.

From the end of 1893 competition on the Gozo run appeared. This took the form of a small steamer built also in Scotland, named PRINCESS MELITA, owned by G.P. Sammut & Co, which arrived at Malta on 15th September. She was a product of Scott of Kinghorn, Fife and had been launched with steam-up for her trials on 28th August, 1893. She sailed from Burntisland (the nearest port to her builder's yard) on 1st September, passing through the English Channel 3 days later. During this period of competition, it was not uncommon for the rival owners to offer inducements to their male passengers to travel with them, by providing either a free cigar or a tot of whisky.

During the period March - July, 1895, GLENEAGLES was chartered by the Maltese Goverment as a trawler to investigate the feasibility of creating a fishing and shrimp industry based on the islands. However, although the catches were plentiful, the trawling gear suffered serious damage because of the nature of the seabed, and the venture was abandoned. During this time LADY DOWNSHIRE carried out the Gozo mail sailings, and it is believed that summer relief between 1895 and 1897 was provided by the locally owned CONCETTA (1884).

As well as carrying the mails, GLENEAGLES on occasions made excursions round Malta, and also assisted vessels in distress. On 1st March, 1898 one of these occasions arose when a ship's boat from s.s. CURFEW (built 1888, 1,949 tons) arrived at Gozo with the news that the vessel was disabled some 120 miles NE of Gozo. GLENEAGLES was despatched to tow her in, and this she did with the assistance of the naval tug SAMPSON next day.

In 1897 further competition appeared in the form of a steamer named PIEMONTE, owned by Francesco Pace. She was somewhat larger than GLENEAGLES and was noted as having 16 cabins for the comfort of her passengers. However, although she received a subsidy of £500 per annum, this additional service did not last long and the vessel was sold to Italian owners in 1901.

In June, 1904, G.P. Sammut & Co with PRINCESS MELITA (1893) took over the mail contract from Gollcher & Sons, although GLENEAGLES continued to run as a passenger and cargo vessel on the route. With passenger traffic building up, during the summer holiday periods between 1904 and 1910, the tug DOLLY (1891) often was pressed into service as a relief vessel, as by this time LADY DOWNSHIRE had been sold, leaving PRINCESS MELITA and GLENEAGLES the only regular passenger steamers on the Gozo run.

PRINCESS MELITA lying off Mgarr

In May, 1913, Gollcher's acquired 21/64th shares in PRINCESS MELITA, and became managing owners of that steamer in October of the same year, virtually eliminating the competition on the route. However, with the outbreak of hostilities in August, 1914, GLENEAGLES was requistioned by the Royal Navy as an examination vessel, her duties being to direct merchant ships to enter Marsaxlokk Bay for quarantine purposes before entering Grand Harbour, so PRINCESS MELITA was left to carry on the Gozo sailings by herself. In February, 1916, the shares in PRINCESS MELITA held by Gollcher's were sold to Colonel Alexander Mattei, who became her new owner.

On the termination of the war in November, 1918, GLENEAGLES was returned to Gollcher's, but it is not known whether she resumed sailings to Gozo, although it seems unlikely. With the death in 1918 of Vincenza Gollcher, widow of the firm's founder, the need to settle estate duty and other debts arose, and GLENEAGLES was sold to other local owners for service in the Eastern Mediterranean. This left PRINCESS MELITA the only regular steamer on the route, but this was not to remain so for long. In 1922 the Malta S.S. Co was formed by a group of local businessmen, and they acquired two steamers in 1923, SIR FILIPPO SCEBERRAS (1892) (renamed WEMBLEY in 1924) and ANDREA BAFILE (1912) (renamed immediately GOLLY). Both these vessels had interesting histories, the former having been built as a trawler for Hull owners, later sold to Spain and then passed to the Italian Navy as a minesweeper before being acquired. Due to a clerical error, when she was re-registered under the British flag in 1923, she was issued with a second Official Number, something that has not happened too often — normally a vessel reverts to its original Official Number should it return to the British register at any time. The latter vessel had been built in Japan as a trawler before becoming the Italian patrol vessel G27. The arrival of these two vessels re-introduced competition on the Gozo run, but with the death of Colonel Mattei in 1923, and the subsequent sale of PRINCESS MELITA for breaking up, the mail contract passed to the new company.

Gozitan boats loading passengers from the shore at Mgarr prior to 1930

The question of improving the facilities at Mgarr was brought up again in June, 1924 by Lord Strickland (who headed the ruling Constitutional Party at that time), so as to eliminate the need to transfer passengers and goods from the steamer to the shore by small boat. After much delay, money was finally provided for the project and the first block of the new breakwater and pier extension was laid by the Bishop of Gozo on 23rd June, 1929. The new pier was completed under the newly elected Nationalist Administration in 1931, at a total cost of £19,000, and this allowed steamers to berth alongside to discharge their loads on to a quay — this quay is now incorporated as the inner berths of the present pier, with the breakwater being extended to form the present outer berths and car ramp. The original quay was shorter than planned, however, as the result of protests of the local Gozitan boatmen, who feared that a longer quay would ruin their business altogether.

The construction of roads on the islands advanced over the years, and by 1930 a surfaced road existed between Valletta and Marfa, at the Northern point of the island of Malta. This stretch of water could be stormy in winter, but with a powered vessel, could easily be crossed in less than 30 minutes. Up till now any passenger having made his way to Marfa by horse transport, then had to depend on the willingness of a Gozitan fisherman to come over and collect him. With the introduction of public service buses to Marfa, there was an obvious need to provide a passenger steamer service to connect with the bus, and such a service was initially performed by a fishing vessel, a motor "luzzi" owned by a St Paul's Bay fisherman. However, this was only for a short time, after which Bernardo Zammit placed his steam launch LADY STRICKLAND (1887), an ex-War Department vessel, on the run. She did not prove large enough for the task, so Zammit bought the Royal Navy tank vessel HELPFUL (1902), converted her for commercial service (including the carriage of a few cars), and renamed her KING OF ENGLAND. This larger vessel came into service in November, 1933, and remained on the route until 1937. When she was not available, she was relieved by either LADY STRICKLAND or DUKE OF GLOUCESTER (1932), this latter vessel also undertaking additional sailings as necessary, but neither of these vessels were capable of carrying cars. The result of the introduction of this new service for passengers, was a great reduction in the numbers carried out of Grand Harbour, and WEMBLEY was taken out of service in 1934. Malta S.S. Co finally went out of business in 1937. Only cargo sailings were then operated between Grand Harbour and Mgarr by the smaller steamer FRANCO (1891) owned by Albert Borg, but subsequently she was joined by the KING OF ENGLAND on this route.

At the beginning of 1937, the Postal Authorities decided that it would be more practical if the mails for Gozo were despatched via Marfa instead of Grand Harbour. The contract for this new service was won by Orazia Mizzi and others, who later formed themselves into the Gozo Mail Co, and they purchased in September, 1937 the Scarborough excursion motor vessel ROYAL LADY (1934). With her glasswork protected by boarding, and her decks stacked with 46 x 40-gallon barrels of oil fuel (to increase her normal tankage of 1,000 gallons), she sailed from Scarborough on 29th September, 1937 under the command of Captain Mizzi her new owner, with Scarborough's Captain L. Simms as mate, and a crew of 9. She arrived in Grand Harbour on 12th October having made the trip non-stop. Her first sailing to Gozo was at 1.30 p.m. on Saturday, 30th October, 1937 when she left Customs House Quay for Mgarr, and on her arrival there was blessed by the Bishop of Gozo. She commenced regular sailings between Mgarr and Marfa on 1st November, and was an immediate success, with her much improved passenger accommodation. She continued to maintain these sailings until immediately prior to the outbreak of World War II in September, 1939, when she was time-chartered by the Royal Navy as an examination vessel. She was subsequently requisitioned as such from February, 1940 until the following August, after which she was returned to her owners (the Mediterranean was by then closed to merchant shipping) to maintain the mail contract again — this had for the summer months been taken over by the small schooner MARIE GORGETTE (later sunk on 29th December, 1941 in an air attack in which 5 lives were lost). During the other periods when ROYAL LADY was not available, she was replaced by the small tug IS-SAJJED (which was herself sunk in Grand Harbour in 1942 as the result of enemy action), and on occasions even local Gozitan fishing vessels had to be pressed into service.

ROYAL LADY off Scarborough

The Mediterranean became the centre of much military and naval activity from the summer of 1940 onwards, and when the Luftwaffe moved into Sicily during January, 1941, the bombing of the islands intensified, the earlier attacks by the Italian Air Force being insignificant in comparison. The air defences of the islands at that time were much below strength, being 42 heavy A.A. guns, 60 light A.A. guns and 3 fighter squadrons short. Re-inforcements of aircraft were flown off carriers to the West of Malta, first in April, 1941 followed again in May and June of the same year. Fortunately the Luftwaffe left Sicily during June, 1941 for service on the Russian front so the islands had a respite for a short time. By January, 1941 the islands only had 7 months supplies of food, fuel and ammunition, with no prospects of further supplies reaching the islands until the summer, so rationing had to be introduced in March, 1941. No major convoy reached the islands until one sailed in from the West in July, 1941 and this then gave the islands sufficient supplies to last until March, 1942. The return of the Luftwaffe to Sicily in December, 1941, and the fact that Malta's strategic position became more vital as the German Afrika Korps advanced into Egypt in early 1942, caused more intensive bombing in an effort to neutralise the island fortress. In April, 1942, some 7,000 tons of bombs were dropped, killing 200 and injuring some 1,000 people, and it was only the use of caves as shelters that saved greater casualties.

KING OF ENGLAND was involved at this time in a dangerous mission. A further attempt to supply the islands was made by the Royal Navy in March, 1942 and amongst the vessels to make this run was the Royal Fleet Auxiliary BRECONSHIRE (built 1939, 9,776 tons), part of her cargo being precious fuel oil. When only 8 miles from Malta she was disabled in a bombing attack but was finally towed into Marsaxlokk Bay but 2 days later was sunk by further bombing. In an attempt to recover the oil, KING OF ENGLAND was sent round from Grand Harbour and defying attacks by the Luftwaffe, she managed to salvage much of the oil fuel onboard BRECONSHIRE, pumping it out barrel by barrel to bring it back to Grand Harbour.

As well as attacking Valletta, the Grand Harbour and surrounding towns, the Luftwaffe was a constant threat to all vessels moving at sea. Mgarr was attacked on several occasions, and ROYAL LADY was machine-gunned on 4th May, 1942 as she lay at the quay, resulting in 2 members of her crew being killed. Three days later in another attack, ROYAL LADY was sunk by bombing, together with the fishing boats CONCETTA MADRE (No 36) and SAN ANTONIO (No 45). FRANCO, also at that time lying at Mgarr, was damaged and again on 10th May. The wreckage of ROYAL LADY was dispersed after the war.

The wreckage of **ROYAL LADY** at Mgarr *(Michael Grima)*

The repeated attacks during daylight had already resulted in vessels only moving at night, and the withdrawal of all sailings from Grand Harbour, but from May, 1942 even daylight sailings to Marfa were withdrawn. FRANCO took over the Marfa sailings and was acquired by the Gozo Mail Co in 1943 as a replacement for the loss of their ROYAL LADY. FRANCO was assisted in the task of providing communications to and from Gozo by local boats. Only the timely arrival of Spitfire and Hurricane fighter aircraft (flown off from aircraft carriers steaming to the West of Malta) saved the islands from suffering even more, and for gallantry, the islands were awarded the George Cross on 13th September, 1942. Because of the heavy losses suffered by merchant ships attempting to make the passage to Malta, food, fuel and supplies generally were extremely short during the early part of 1942, and it was only the arrival of a convoy in August, 1942 that relieved this desperate situation.

Subsequently with the Allied Armies landing in North Africa, the defeat of the Afrika Korps in Tunisia, and the withdrawal of Italy from the War, the pressure on Malta was eliminated, allowing Allied merchant ships once again to pass through the Mediterranean without hindrance.

As the tide of War moved away from the Mediterranean, life began to return to normal in the islands, and KING OF ENGLAND, now owned by Galzamhil Co Ltd (a combination of the names of her owners, Galea, Zammit and Hill), returned to the Marfa sailings in October, 1944 and to augment those offered by FRANCO. The mail contract, held for some 10 years by the Gozo Mail Co, came up for renewal in 1947, and it passed to Joseph Gasan.

Joseph Gasan was no stranger to operating steamer services, as he had been involved in the Malta — Syracuse mail sailings between 1923 and 1936. In anticipation of obtaining the contract, Gasan had purchased in September, 1947 the twin-screw yacht MIGRANTE (1927), a vessel of 357 tons, employed on anti-submarine duties during the War as H.M. Yacht FY019. Work was put in hand to convert this vessel for commercial service, but this proved to be a slow job, and in fact it was not until July, 1950 that she came into service as BANCINU. Meantime, in order to meet his contract, Gasan first chartered the motor launch CYGNET (1934), but she proved too small and he was forced to charter various vessels. Next was NANRIDI (1943), a converted motor minesweeper, but as her owners (A. Theuma & P.P. Moore) had no certified master to command her, a Grand Harbour pilot (at great expense!) had to be employed as master. This high cost could not be absorbed and after only a few weeks, NANRIDI was withdrawn and another converted minesweeper LORD STRICKLAND (1942), owned by Anglia Shipping Co Ltd, was chartered instead. Her stay on the sailings was also short and in January, 1948 her place was taken by the Grand Harbour steam ferry EMILY P (1914), owned by the National Steam Ferry Co, a firm in which Gollcher & Sons had a major interest. This vessel was only a small passenger launch and not capable of carrying cargo. However, in March, 1948 a larger steamer, named SUPPLY (1910) was chartered from Coleiro Navigation Co Ltd, which although capable of carrying cargo, had little accommodation for passengers. KING OF ENGLAND was withdrawn from the Marfa route in May, 1948 and returned to Grand Harbour — Mgarr sailings, where she joined the motor yacht HANINI (1926), which had been on this route since about 1945, owned by Magro Bros, Mgarr. This latter vessel was only suitable for passengers and a small amount of cargo.

SUPPLY continued to operate the Marfa sailings from Mgarr on charter to Gasan during 1948/49, but with the conversion of MIGRANTE no nearer completion, and the fact that cargo space on SUPPLY was limited with no possibility of carrying cars, Gasan purchased in May, 1949 an ex-Royal Navy minesweeper, similar to NANRIDI and LORD STRICKLAND that he had earlier chartered, and converted her for commercial service. She was given the name CALYPSO G (1942) and placed on the sailings in March, 1950 in place of SUPPLY. The latter was then used as a tank vessel — she was originally a water carrier for the Royal Navy — and carried water to Comino, returning to Grand Harbour with wine from Mgarr, for her owners who were in the wine industry. She was at the time renamed ROSINA M.

BANCINU at Marfa Pier

CALYPSO G was not to remain on the service long, as in July, 1950 (after only 4 months service), Gasan sold her at a good price to a Trust, who transferred her to the Compagnie Oceanographique Francaise, Nice. She was subsequently converted to an ocean survey and undersea research vessel, the letter G was dropped from her name, and she is now better known as the vessel commanded by Jacques Cousteau, her picture being seen in many films and television programmes all over the world. The sale of CALYPSO G and the fact that no suitable replacement was immediately available for the Marfa sailings, produced an outcry from the public, as well as the Postal Authorities. MIGRANTE was still not converted and Gasan had to charter the auxiliary ketch MAID OF PINTO (1944), normally working as a salvage vessel. Her passenger accommodation was totally inadequate (if not non-existant), and Gasan found himself under much adverse criticism for his action. However, at long last in July, 1950 BANCINU (ex-MIGRANTE) became available for service, and took over the Mgarr — Marfa sailings from MAID OF PINTO. BANCINU was a smart little steamer, and was a vast improvement from the passengers' point of view. She was only basically a passenger carrying vessel and could not uplift cars or other than a small amount of cargo. When BANCINU had to go into dock for her annual overhaul, as Gasan had no relief vessel, Magro's HANINI took over the sailings and the latter's passenger sailings from Grand Harbour were suspended for the periods she carried out this relief. In 1951 the 49-year old KING OF ENGLAND went to the breakers (as did the even older LADY STRICKLAND (1887)) and HANINI was left on the Grand Harbour route alone, supported by local auxiliary schooners who carried all the general cargo and agricultural products.

No further changes took place until 1956, when with the mail contract between Mgarr and Marfa due for renewal in the next year, various owners made their preparations in anticipation of being successful. In July, Gasan acquired yet another ex-Royal Navy minesweeper and took steps to convert her for commercial service, mainly as a possible relief for BANCINU, as HANINI was totally inadequate in size and not very pleasant to sail on because of engine noise and vibration. In September 1955, Magro Bros had bought a similar vessel from the Royal Navy and also took steps to convert her, with the object of her replacing HANINI. Magro's completed the conversion and, renamed QUEEN OF PEACE (1942), she took over the sailings from HANINI in May, 1956. QUEEN OF PEACE was fitted with ramps to allow cars and tankers to be loaded on her aft deck, as by this time the demand to move vehicles between the islands was increasing — hoisting cars over the side onto the deck of a schooner was not very effective, very slow, and the number that could be carried was very limited.

Gasan's conversion again took a long time to complete but finally on 22nd January, 1957 the vessel, named PINU (1942) took over the sailings from BANCINU. Unfortunately during the night of 23rd January, 1957, when BANCINU was lying tied up at Mgarr, a strong Westerly gale blew up and the vessel broke away from her moorings. She was driven onto the rocky coastline and the only person onboard at the time, the night watchman, was lost. BANCINU lay on the rocks half submerged and badly holed until 10th February, when the Royal Navy salvage ship UPLIFTER raised her and towed her to Grand Harbour. However, with the mail contract due for renewal, and the time it would take to repair the damage, to say nothing of the cost, Gasan left the damaged vessel as she was until it was established who was to have the new mail contract. Meantime the sailings to Marfa were maintained by PINU until 30th October, 1957, when, as Gasan had been unsuccessful in retaining the contract, both PINU and the damaged BANCINU were sold. Joseph Gasan ceased to own ships and concentrated on his other business activities including that of main distribution agent for Ford Motors in Malta. He died at the age of 85 on 3rd July, 1976, and Gasan Enterprises is now controlled by his son.

BANCINU stranded on the rocks of Mgarr — February, 1957 *(Viktor Wickman)*

The successful contender for the new mail contract was Magro & Zammit. This was a partnership between the Magro Bros, Gozitan merchants and owners of schooners and QUEEN OF PEACE, and Ewkaristiko Zammit, another Gozitan merchant who had been involved from the Second World War years in supplying the Royal Navy with vegetables and eggs from Gozo. The contract became effective from 1st November, 1957 and called for the carriage of not only passengers and mail, but also at least 6 cars per trip between Mgarr and Marfa. The partners immediately commenced looking for a suitable vessel to undertake this task and were successful in finding the Thames pleasure motor vessel CRESTED EAGLE (1938). This vessel left the Thames on 20th November, 1957 in tow of the tug ENGLISHMAN (built 1945 - 716 tons), and arrived safely in Grand Harbour on 5th December. She was taken in hand for certain modifications including the provision of ramps to load cars on her aft deck, the removal of part of the superstructure to give more deck space to accommodate these cars, a new and larger wheelhouse and a higher prow to protect her forecastle from heavy seas. While this work was being carried out, the service was commenced on 1st November by Magro's QUEEN OF PEACE, the latter vessel's place on the Grand Harbour service meantime being taken by the schooner SAN BERT, owned by Magro Bros.

CRESTED EAGLE had been built in the same yard, and for the same owners, as ROYAL LADY (1934), and had originally been named NEW ROYAL LADY (although locally known at Scarborough as ROYAL LADY II). When she was sold for service in 1947 on the Firth of Forth she was renamed ROYAL LADY but on her transfer to the Thames to operate cruises round the London Docks, she took the name CRESTED EAGLE. By the time that she appeared on the Marfa run on 2nd June, 1958, she had been renamed IMPERIAL EAGLE, and her arrival then allowed QUEEN OF PEACE to revert to her normal Grand Harbour sailings. IMPERIAL EAGLE remained on this crossing until October, 1967, when the mail contract expired but over these 9 years she proved a most reliable vessel. As will be seen, she was to serve Malta for many years yet to come.

IMPERIAL EAGLE as **NEW ROYAL LADY OFF** off Scarborough

A further alternative to either travelling to Gozo by IMPERIAL EAGLE via Marfa, or QUEEN OF PEACE via Grand Harbour was the introduction in 1964 of the hydrofoil DELPHIN, bought from Yugo-Slavia, and put into service between Grand Harbour and Mgarr. This new service only lasted for 2 summer seasons, when because of the unreliability of the craft and the lack of capital, the hydrofoil was laid-up, and eventually in 1968 sold to Italian owners for service elsewhere.

Hydrofoil **DELPHIN** passing Maltese National Lines **MALCOLM PACE** (1947) *(Vicktor Wickman)*

The year 1967 saw competition appear again on the Grand Harbour sailings. In October, 1966, Zammit (of the Magro & Zammit partnership) acquired his first vessel. This was the ex-coastal minelayer MINER VI (1942), and she was taken in hand so that she could carry water to Comino (there was a shortage on that island where large numbers of visitors were now landing) in place of ROSINA M. As well as carrying passengers and cargo, she was able to carry a few vehicles on her fore deck, the necessary ramps having been fitted. On her upper deck bench seats were provided for 450 passengers. She came into service in 1967 as MINOR EAGLE and was hardly recognisable from her original self. Her original engines were retained, and later a sampson post and derrick was fitted to allow lifting of heavy items of cargo onto her fore deck. The water contract terminated in 1970, when ROSINA M (ex-SUPPLY) took over the task again carrying water to Comino and wine from Gozo to Grand Harbour.

The mail contract was due to come up again for renewal at the end of October, 1967. Trading conditions had changed considerably since 1957, with the number of road vehicles wishing to cross to Gozo having greatly increased in numbers and size, so the new contract called for a vessel that could carry at least 30 cars per trip. Three tenders were received, and Ewkaristiko Zammit (as E. Zammit & Sons) was successful in securing the 10-year contract from 1st November, 1967 — the firm of Magro & Zammit had also submitted an offer but this was not successful.

When the date of the new contract came, IMPERIAL EAGLE carried on the service as Zammit's had still to purchase a vessel suitable for the task. It was not until December, 1967 that they found and purchased the Norwegian car and passenger ferry JYLLAND (1943) — she cost them £M100,000. JYLLAND had originally been built for the United States Navy as submarine chaser (escort) PCE 828, but some months later was transferred to the Royal Navy as a patrol vessel and renamed H.M.S. KILBRIDE. She had been returned to the USN in December, 1946 and in February, 1948 sold to a Norwegian company. Converted for use as a car ferry between Kristiansand and Hirtshals (Denmark), she was renamed JYLLAND (Jutland) in 1949 when she entered commercial service. Michael Zammit — the second eldest son and a master mariner — was despatched to collect this vessel from Kristiansand. He sailed from that port on 19th January, 1968, put into the Tyne on the 21st, and Plymouth on the 24th for fuel, before setting out from that last port on the 25th bound for Malta,

JYLLAND approaching Marfa Pier *(G.H. Somner)*

where JYLLAND arrived safely on 1st February, 1968. She was taken in hand at Marsa for modifications to meet local requirements and took over the sailings from IMPERIAL EAGLE on the afternoon of 20th March, having during the morning made berthing trials at Shipwreck Promenade, St Paul's Bay (an alternative berth in the event of strong winds on the Northern Coast), Marfa and Mgarr. It was only by the skillful handling of the vessel by her new master, Captain Publius Scicluna, that these trials were achieved as the St Paul's berth was too short and low for such a large vessel, and that at Mgarr allowed only 5 feet to spare when QUEEN OF PEACE was also berthed there. JYLLAND turned out to be a most handy vessel for the service, with plenty of power, well able to cope with the winter gales met with on the crossing, and with capacity for 32 cars.

IMPERIAL EAGLE was then laid-up at Marsa, pending the winding-up of the partnership of Magro's and Zammit, but this proved to be a slow and painful process. Magro Bros continued to operate the sailings from Grand Harbour, but QUEEN OF PEACE was now some 24 years old, of wooden construction, with her hull calling for constant repair. Magro's were interested in acquiring IMPERIAL EAGLE to replace her, but as the proceedings continued to drag on through the courts, they decided in 1970 to purchase another vessel to relieve QUEEN OF PEACE. This was the 481-ton Norwegian passenger motor ship JESMAR (1953), which was ideally suited for operating a passenger service to Gozo, but was not capable of loading cars, except by lifting them from the quayside by derrick, unless extensive modifications were made to her. However, by the time JESMAR arrived in Maltese waters, the court case over IMPERIAL EAGLE had been settled and Magro Bros were able to buy her. IMPERIAL EAGLE then joined MINOR EAGLE on sailings from Grand Harbour, and QUEEN OF PEACE was laid-up at Marsa Creek. JESMAR then became surplus, although she did in fact make one excursion to Gozo on 22nd July, 1970, before being laid-up, as it had been found that her freeboard was too high for her to use the pier at Mgarr, and any modifications to reduce the problem of disembarking/embarking passengers there would have been uneconomic. She was eventually sold in 1973 for service in the North Sea involving oil survey work.

QUEEN OF PEACE remained laid up until 1975 when she was sold to other owners. She was docked for overhaul but on her trials afterwards she unfortunately hit a quay and her stern was severely damaged. In November, 1976 she had been repaired but still lay in Marsa Creek, and it was not until early in 1977 that she went to sea again sailing between Italy and Cyprus. She foundered in heavy seas about 25th November, 1977 in the Gulf of Sirte with the loss of three of her crew.

JYLLAND maintained frequent sailings both summer and winter on the Marfa run, but during her first summer season in 1968 it soon became apparent that her capacity of 32 cars was inadequate to meet peak demands. Zammit's decided that they would have to acquire a vessel with a greater capacity, but because of the limitations dictated by the depth of water at the quays, and the length of vessel that these quays could accommodate, the choice was restricted, especially as any vessel selected must be capable of battling with the rough waters of the Comino Channel in Winter.

This time a vessel was located in Holland, where as the result of the construction of new polders (dams), the need for ferries between the islands was decreasing. One of these surplus ferries was the ro-ro PRINS HENDRIK, built in 1932 for the Flushing to Breskins service across the Westerschelde, and capable of carrying 35/40 cars and 1,300 passengers. She had had rather an "under-seas" career, having been sunk by the Dutch Authorities in May, 1940 at Breskins, when the German Army had invaded Holland, raised 3 months later, only to be laid-up until scuttled once again by the German Authorities in October, 1944 in the harbour mouth of Flushing when the Allied Armies approached. There she lay until June, 1947 when she was once more raised and sent to her builders for repairs. She returned to service on 10th December, 1949 and remained on the ferry service until 1968 — her service then amounted to 27 years "afloat", 4 years laid-up or under repair, 2 years 8 months "under sea"! In the course

PRINS HENDRIK as rebuilt in 1948 *(J.J. Steketee)*

of her career she was lengthened, re-engined, and acquired a new superstructure. Zammit's bought this vessel and on 28th March, 1969 she left Flushing in tow of the tug FAIRPLAY XI (built 1963, 173 tons), passed Gibraltar on 5th April, and arrived in Grand Harbour on 10th April. A few days later she sailed to Mgarr and took over the summer sailings from JYLLAND, the latter being held in reserve in case of mechanical failure and employed during the winter in place of PRINS HENDRIK, which having been built for service on inland waters was flat bottomed, and therefore not suitable to cope with rough weather in the open sea. In 1970 PRINS HENDRIK was renamed CALYPSO LAND.

With the introduction of larger and additional vessels, the quay at Mgarr became too small. There was a need to provide a ro-ro berth to load and discharge cars (especially now that CALYPSO LAND could more easily load vehicles in this fashion), and also to provide more shelter and protection to vessels from gale force winds when moored to the quay. Work was authorised in 1970 by the Nationalist administration (then in power) for a new breakwater, lengthening of the existing quay, and construction of a new quay (including a ro-ro berth) on the line of the existing breakwater. The contract for this work was given to an Italian firm, and they commenced to form the new breakwater by positioning large blocks of stone for which they used the crane barge PYGMALION and the tug CREO (ex-FRISKY, ex-EMPIRE RITA). All the work was completed by 1973 but because of a dispute concerning the contract conditions between the Italian firm and the Socialist administration (now in power), the barge and tug became permanent fixtures in the harbour pending a settlement.

By 1973 trade had increased to such an extent that a still larger vessel was required to cope with the summer traffic, and also to be able to load the larger commercial vehicles that wanted to use the ferry. Later that year Zammit's looked again towards Holland for the source of such a vessel. This time they found a ro-ro ferry named DORDRECHT, which had in fact been a "running mate" of PRINS HENDRIK from 1936. DORDRECHT had been built in 1933 but she had been lengthened, re-engined and "re-styled" in such a way in 1955/56 that she had the appearance of a much more modern vessel. She was capable of loading about 80 cars and carrying 600 passengers, and like CALYPSO LAND was driven by a screw at each end. She was some 36 feet longer and drew some 2 feet more water than CALYPSO LAND, which was just within the limits of the pier at Marfa, but the Government of Malta indicated that a new berth at Cirkewwa, about 1 mile West of Marfa would be constructed in the near future, to give better facilities for the larger ferry, so the purchase went ahead. DORDRECHT was dry-docked in Holland and renamed MELITA LAND early in 1974.

MELITA LAND as **DORDRECHT** after lengthening (but not re-engined) in 1955 *(J.J. Steketee)*

In February, 1974, MELITA LAND, commanded by Michael Zammit, commenced her voyage out to Malta under her own power. She had been built for service on inland waters, and a voyage of this duration in winter conditions was to prove quite an ordeal for both ship and crew. All went well until she entered the Bay of Biscay when under gale conditions, engine trouble developed and she found herself adrift without power. Fortunately the Dutch tug ENGELAND (built 1968, 229 tons) was in the vicinity and took her in tow, both arriving at Bilbao, Spain on 15th February. As repairs could not be carried out there, it was arranged that the tug (which was proceeding South anyway to pick-up a tow), would continue the tow to Gibraltar, whilst spares were flown out to that point from England. Gibraltar was reached on 25th February, repairs to the engine were carried out, and MELITA LAND sailed from Gibraltar once again under her own power for Grand Harbour, where she arrived on 5th March. She took over

MARSALFORN
VICTORIA
NADUR
MGARR
GOZO
COM
CIRKEWWA
MARFA
PARADISE BAY
MELLIEHA
N
MALTA

THE MALTESE ISLANDS

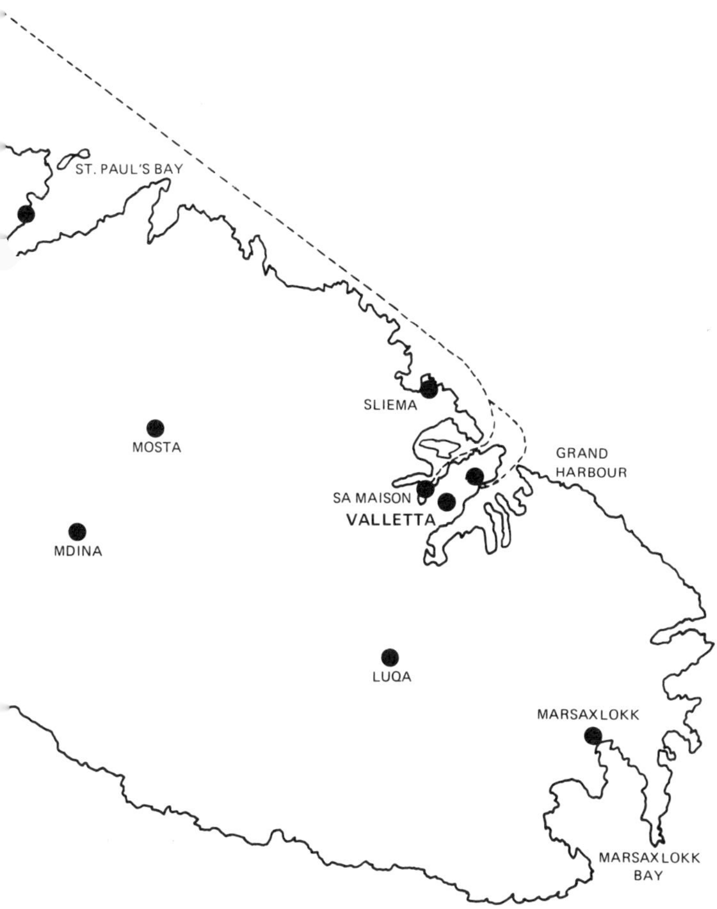

the summer sailings between Mgarr and Marfa on 16th June, 1974 and very quickly proved her worth. However, on occasions, because of her length and the depth of water that she drew, she found herself in difficulties at Marfa quay, which forced her to use the rather poor facilities at Paradise Bay, further along the Northern Coast, normally used when strong Northerly winds were blowing. She also was used to carry heavy commercial vehicles or other heavy loads direct from Grand Harbour when such a need arose.

For some years from 1973 a standard pattern of sailings was maintained with those between Gozo and Grand Harbour being made daily, Monday to Saturday, by IMPERIAL EAGLE (now nearly 40 years old) and MINOR EAGLE, departure times being 5.0/6.0. a.m. from Mgarr and 12.0/1.0. p.m. from Lascaris Wharf, Grand Harbour. These two vessels were supplemented by local motor schooners which carried bulk commodities

MARIE GEORGETTE outward bound for Gozo *(Viktor Wickman)*

such as fertilisers etc to Gozo. The Gozo/Marfa sailings (up to seven per day in Summer, reducing to four in Winter) were maintained by CALYPSO LAND or JYLLAND in winter, with the larger capacity MELITA LAND being used during the peak holiday months June — September in place of JYLLAND. During the summers of 1973/74 JYLLAND made sailings to Syracuse, Sicily but this did not prove successful.

In 1976 MINOR EAGLE, now 34 years old, was fitted with new and more powerful engines, which reduced her passage time from 2 hours to 1 hour 10 minutes. She was renamed COMINOLAND to bring her nomenclature into line with other vessels owned by Zammit & Sons. Whilst she was being refitted her place was taken by a small launch named COMINOTTO, an ex-Royal Naval motor torpedo boat with a capacity for about 80 tons of cargo.

Work on the new berth at Cirkewwa (Marfa Point), although started in 1974 under the direct control of the Government, was not however completed until 1977. However, on one occasion it was used before its official opening when on 3rd November, 1976 CALYPSO LAND developed engine trouble whilst at Marfa pier, and JYLLAND was put into service at short notice to take the last sailing of the day from Malta. As JYLLAND was unable to use Marfa pier, she had to use the new quay (although not the ro-ro berth). The new berth, which is more adequate than Marfa pier, nevertheless is still open to Northerly winds and because of this, can prove to be difficult to use in gale force conditions.

The Comino Channel ferry contract became due for renewal on 15th May, 1978, but in the light of the nationalisation of other transport undertakings in Malta, it was anticipated that the ferry service might also be taken over by the Government. However, as tenders for the ferry service were only called for during April, 1978 to cover the period of the next 5 years, any new contender for the contract would have to procure a suitable vessel in a number of days, so it seemed likely that only Zammit's could possibly continue to operate the sailings. The conditions of the new contract were much stiffer than those currently in force, and because of this and the fact their vessels could not be modified to meet the requirements regarding safety and reliability, Zammit's did not submit a tender. This left the Government in a predicament, and to allow time to consider the situation, they asked Zammit's to continue the sailings after the contract expired, for a period of 6 months. It was rumoured at this time that Sea Malta (the Government controlled shipping company) might take over the running of all ferries, and there were high hopes that this organisation would be able to provide a higher standard of safety, a more frequent and speedier service at a reasonable cost to the travelling public.

When the 6 month period was passed in November, it was belatedly announced that as none of the tenders received had met the conditions laid down, new applications were being asked for, with a closure date of 15th December, 1978. Again this gave no real time for any new company to organise itself and acquire the necessary ship, so this time the Government chartered MELITA LAND from Zammit's to carry on the sailings — they had little choice in the matter if some sort of sailings were to be maintained meantime.

It was, therefore, no real suprise when in January, 1979, it was announced that a new company was to be formed, with the help of the Malta Development Corporation, to operate sailings to Gozo both from Cirkewwa and Grand Harbour. The name of the company was to be Gozo Channel Co Ltd, the directors of which were to be two Government nominees and two nominated by Sea Malta. The Danish registered car ferry ROTNA (1962), of 2,301 tons gross, was quickly purchased at a cost of £M900,000, and she arrived in Grand Harbour on 28th January, 1979, from Belgium, where she had been overhauled, painted and renamed GHAWDEX (the Maltese for Gozo). This vessel, with a length of 289 feet, was 58 feet longer than MELITA LAND, and was the largest vessel ever to be employed on ferry services in Malta, being capable of carrying some 1,200 passengers and 120 cars at a speed of 18 knots. This large vessel required a suitable berth in Grand Harbour to enable her to load vehicles, and at Mgarr it would be necessary to remove part of the ramp to allow her bow door to be used, but as neither of these two requirements could be met immediately, GHAWDEX could not be introduced into service. Hurried arrangements were made to construct a suitable vehicle loading berth at Sa Maison, Pieta Creek but it was not until 30th March, 1979 (from a berth still not completed and allowing bow loading only) that she made her first sailing to Mgarr, where the necessary modifications had been made. Thereafter she sailed twice daily, departing from Sa Maison at 9.0 a.m. and 2.0 p.m., with return sailings from Mgarr at 11.0 a.m. and 5.0 p.m.

GHAWDEX entering Grand Harbour, passing Sea Malta's Qormi (1973) outward bound *(Michael Cassar)*

No sooner had this service been introduced, when criticism was levelled at the Company by the Gozitans. Their high hopes of a better and more conveniently timed service were dashed, as the sailing times did not meet Gozo's domestic needs (an early departure to Malta), nor the needs of the tourist (a later return time). At the same time, fares were increased by about 100% in order that the Company could meet the heavy capital costs of acquiring the vessel and constructing or modifying the berths. To add fuel to the fire of controversy, within a day of commencing her sailings, GHAWDEX became the centre of further doubts as to her suitability for maintaining a regular service between the islands. On 31st March arrangements had been made so that Gozitans could have the opportunity of attending the celebrations at Vittoriosa (on Malta) to cover the departure of the last British Forces stationed in Malta. GHAWDEX carried nearly 1,000 passengers to Valletta on her scheduled 5.0 p.m. run from Mgarr, and it was intended that she would make a special return sailing at 2.30 a.m. the following morning (1st April) to get the Gozitan passengers back home after the celebrations had finished. Unfortunately rough weather blew up with a gale from the North East, so because of this, the master decided to remain tied-up until conditions improved — GHAWDEX had of course been designed and constructed for service in relatively shallow sheltered waters of the Baltic, so she would not be a very good seaboat in a wild Mediterranean storm! She was still in port at 6.45 a.m. but under pressure from the passengers who wanted to get home, the master put to sea, only to return hastily some hours later after being hit by heavy seas when approaching the Comino Channel.

It was not until late in June, 1979 that the permanent berth at Pieta Creek allowed GHAWDEX to berth stern first, and so permit loading of heavy vehicles and the use of her "through" loading facilities by the use of the bow door at Mgarr. Unfortunately containers could not be loaded due to a lack of headroom on her car deck. In the first 10 weeks of her service, she carried some 50,000 passengers and 7,200 vehicles (an uplift factor of 14.8% and 21.4% respectively), but with fuel for 280 trips and the wages for 34 crew to be paid for, a much greater volume of traffic was necessary if the ship was to pay her way.

With Zammit's interest in the Comino Channel reduced, employment had to be found for JYLLAND and CALYPSO LAND. During the summer months of 1979 JYLLAND undertook cruises round Malta and Gozo 3 days a week, whilst CALYPSO LAND was employed carrying building materials from Gozo to Comino, where the Government were constructing a piggery. The latter vessel was assisted in this work by DE PAOLA (1951) working out of Grand Harbour. DE PAOLA was previously the Firth of Tay car ferry SCOTSCRAIG but she was now practically unrecognisable as such, her bow section cut off, her superstructure shortened, and her wheelhouse moved aft so that now she had the appearance of a landing craft.

DE PAOLO entering Grand Harbour *(Michael Cassar)*

The summer season of 1979 was not without its difficulties for the ferry services, and as forecast when the schedules were first announced, many tourists on day trips to Gozo found themselves stranded at Mgarr because of over-booking on the last crossing of the day to Cirkewwa, and naturally this caused unfavourable comments from the visitors. The principal reason for this unhappy state of affairs was the high level of fares for passengers and cars on the direct sailings to Grand Harbour, compared with those via Cirkewwa using the ferry and bus, consequently putting pressure on the space on the cheaper route. In an attempt to try and overcome this situation, Gozo Channel Co altered the schedule of GHAWDEX from 11th August, 1979 so that instead of a twice daily run to Mgarr, a single trip was operated from Mgarr at 6.45 a.m. (which Gozitans had always wanted), with a return sailing from Pieta Creek at 9.0 a.m.

(which they did not want). This then made GHAWDEX available to supplement sailings between Mgarr and Cirkewwa currently operated by MELITA LAND unaided. This change resulted in no further complaints from stranded passengers and also reduced the losses sustained by GHAWDEX but of course resulted in a further deterioration in the use of Grand Harbour sailings. Because of her size, there were difficulties in berthing GHAWDEX at both Mgarr and Cirkewwa, and it was obvious that this change could only be of a temporary nature. Certain blasting and dredging work was undertaken at Cirkewwa but even this did not correct the situation.

By the end of the summer season 1979 it was quite apparent that GHAWDEX was never likely to provide a reliable and cheap service between Malta and Gozo, being too large for the amount of traffic offering, too expensive to run, and not really capable of operating in all weathers. Fares had to be increased very dramatically but even so there was a loss of £60,000 in just 9 months, so that it was obvious that she was not a viable proposition and that the Company would have to take drastic action to remedy this situation. From October, 1979, GHAWDEX made only one round trip a day to Mgarr from Sa Maison (out in the morning, back in the late afternoon). MELITA LAND, now no longer on charter to the Gozo Channel Co, continued to operate independently the Comino Channel sailings, berthing again at Marfa pier, initially with 4 sailings per day. However, when regulations were introduced that required that vehicles registered in Malta had to travel on GHAWDEX, whilst only those registered in Gozo could cross on MELITA LAND, Zammit's were forced to reduce the sailings to twice a day.

By the end of 1979 the Gozo Channel Co were actively looking for a purchaser for GHAWDEX, and although Greek owners showed interest in her, no firm offers were received. Meantime the Company themselves were seeking a smaller ship, easier to manoeuvre at Mgarr and Cirkewwa, with lower operating costs, but with the capability of sailing in all but the worst weather conditions, on both the short and long crossings. In December, 1979 they agreed to purchase the Swedish ferry SALTHOLM (1967), and after a rough passage the vessel arrived at Malta on 16th January, 1980. Of 728 tons gross, fitted with a bow door, she was capable of carrying up to 40 cars together with some 400 passengers at a speed of 10 knots. She cost the Company £M200,000 and on arrival she underwent a refit which cost a further £M20,000.

The Maltese Goverment invited the travel trade (on which Malta and Gozo are so dependent) and Zammit & Sons to become shareholders in Gozo Channel Co in January, 1980, with the Government holding 51%, the travel trade 20%, and Zammit & Sons 29%, part of the latter's contribution being the transfer of MELITA LAND to the Company. MELITA LAND appeared in her new owner's colours in February, 1980.

The maiden voyage of MGARR ex-SALTHOLM took place on 8th March, 1980, initially on the Mgarr — Cirkewwa route, but after a few days of "running-in" she relieved GHAWDEX to allow that vessel to have her first overhaul since her purchase some 14 months earlier. When this overhaul had been completed, MGARR reverted to the shorter route again whilst MELITA LAND in turn went in for her annual overhaul. The introduction into service of MGARR at this time was also upset by rough weather and she proved to be no more stable in these conditions than her "running-

MGAAR as SALTHOLM in Grand Harbour *(Michael Cassar)*

mates". With a speed of only 10 knots, her passage time on the Grand Harbour route was longer than IMPERIAL EAGLE (which could still make 12 knots even though 41 years old), and as a result traffic further declined due to these slow and often uncomfortable passages.

MELITA LAND returned from overhaul in June just in time to assist MGARR on the summer sailings across the Comino Channel. During 1980 GHAWDEX, as she had not been sold, resumed her once daily sailing between Sa Maison and Mgarr to meet tourist demands, outwards at 9.30 a.m., returning from Gozo at 5.0 p.m.

Until May, 1980, the inhabitants and visitors staying on Gozo found that they could not attend any evening social events in Malta as the last ferry left Cirkewwa at 7.45 p.m. As an experiment the motor launch CALLBOY, an ex-British War Department vessel, was introduced by Zammit's on a night service, with departures from Cirkewwa at 10.0 p.m., 1.30 a.m. and 4.0 a.m., and although the single fare of £M1.50 was high (compared with the daytime fare of 40c), it was an instant success with the "night birds" of Gozo. Two launches are now employed on this night service.

Regulations came into force that many goods destined for Gozo must be pre-loaded onto trucks so that better use was made of the car deck on GHAWDEX. Nevertheless there remained an over-capacity situation on the Grand Harbour route, and GHAWDEX with her much higher running costs than either IMPERIAL EAGLE or COMINOLAND continued to run at a loss. To reduce the over-capacity situation, the Government ordered that sailings ot the two smaller vessels be suspended from 16th May, 1980. This caused merchants to protest most strongly, as not only was the cost of shipping goods on GHAWDEX much more expensive, but merchants in Gozo were no longer able to ship their fresh vegetables to Malta for the early morning markets (GHAWDEX did not sail until 5.0 p.m. whereas the other vessels sailed in the early hours of the morning), and those in Malta were forced to send their goods down to the quay the previous afternoon or very early in the morning to connect with a 9.0. a.m. sailing instead of a departure at noon or 1.0 p.m.. After strong protests from all quarters, the Government rescinded the suspension after some 6 weeks. However, whilst IMPERIAL EAGLE resumed her sailings, but now with cargo only, COMINOLAND did not, as she had not been paying her way previously. Instead Zammit's sent her for a refit to allow her to undertake twice weekly cruises to Comino renamed JYLLAND II. Because of the lack of support, these cruises were withdrawn after a short time, and JYLLAND II was laid-up at Msida. The cruises were introduced again in 1981 but met with the same fate and JYLLAND II was laid up once again.

JYLLAND II — August, 1980 *(Michael Grima)*

Zammit & Sons had come to agreement early in 1980 for the sale of JYLLAND to Italian owners for service between Capri and Ischia, but because the Italian authorities refused to permit the transfer of the necessary funds, this sale fell through. JYLLAND was therefore available to resume the summer cruises round Malta and Gozo. CALYPSO LAND was again chartered in April to carry building materials to Comino, but by August was laid-up at Marsa. JYLLAND, at the end of a rather disappointing summer season, was laid up at Sliema.

By November, 1980 with light traffic on the Grand Harbour sailings, the Company had no alternative but to lay-up GHAWDEX at Sa Maison, and substitute instead twice-weekly sailings by MGARR, which had lower operating costs. GHAWDEX resumed the daily sailings to Mgarr in March, 1981, but those on Thursdays and Sundays were suspended from 16th June so that the vessel could operate a return sailing to Syracuse, Sicily instead, following the pattern that JYLLAND had run for two summers some years earlier. These sailings are proving highly popular.

Malta remains a firm favourite of tourists of many countries, especially British, and the ferry services between the islands will for this reason always have to face up to having to provide accommodation for large numbers of passengers, cars and coaches during the summer months, whilst there is little traffic to fill the ships during the winter months with only local needs to satisfy. With the improvement in land communications, possibly the answer may lie in concentrating the movement of passengers and goods over the shorter Mgarr — Cirkewwa crossing.

In nearly 100 years since regular ferry sailings have been in operation between Malta and Gozo, there have been many changes in not only vessel types — from sail, to steam and now to motor ship — but with the coming of increased vehicle movements, the method of loading has also had to change — from hoisting onboard, later by side loading, and now roll on/roll off. The story of the inter-island ferries of Malta is a continuing one and will no doubt change in the future to meet the ever altering needs of the traffic between the Maltese islands.

LIST OF MAJOR VESSELS OPERATING MALTA TO GOZO PASSENGER/CAR FERRY SERVICES

Notes

1. The dates following the name are those of when the vessel was on the ferry service.
2. Tonnages are "gt" — gross, and "nt" — net.
3. Dimensions are registered length x beam x depth to main deck of all vessels, in all cases dimensions being to the nearest foot.
4. Horsepower—"hp"—is registered unless otherwise indicated e.g. "bhp"—brake horsepower
5. The ships histories are corrected up to September, 1981

m.v. BANCINU (1950-1957), twin-screw motor yacht
Official Number: 149387. Tonnages 357 gross, 207 net. Dimensions—length: 128 feet x beam: 24 feet x depth: 11 feet — from *1960*, Tonnages: 525gt, 369nt.
Oil engines (2), each 6-cyl, Maschfbk. Augsburg-Nurnberg A.G., Augsburg.

11.1927: Completed by Clyde Shipbuilding & Engineering Co Ltd, Port Glasgow for K.E. Lee Guiness, Greenock as MIGRANT. *1933:* Sold to Cie Generale de Publicite Parisienne S.A., Nice and renamed VICTRIX. *1936:* Renamed MIGRANTE. *9.1939:* Requisitioned by Royal Navy as Armed Yacht FY 019 for anti-submarine duties. *7.1941:* Purchased by Ministry of War Transport for same duties. *1946:* Re-acquired by previous owner. *9.1947:* Acquired by Joseph Gasan, Malta and modifications commenced to convert to a ferry. *7.1950:* Renamed BANCINU and went into service. *23.1.1957:* Broke from moorings at Mgarr in a gale and driven ashore. *10.2.1957:* Salvaged by Royal Navy salvage vessel UPLIFTER and towed to Grand Harbour. *12.1957:* Sold to B. Vasilakis, Piraeus. *1958:* Renamed ATHINAI. *1961:* Sold to Kavounides Shipping Co Ltd, Piraeus and renamed SIRIUS. *1964:* Sold to Saronikos S.A. Maritime Enterprises, Piraeus and renamed V. SPORADES. Still in service.

BANCINU being towed into Grand Harbour after being refloated by H.M. Salvage vessel **UPLIFTER** — February, 1957
(Vicktor Wickman)

p.s. BULLDOG (1859- ?), wooden paddle tug
O.N. 2131. 77gt, 47nt, 80 x 17 x 9 feet
Engine 40hp.

6.1855: Completed at North Shields for Richard Swan, North Shields, and sailed out to Constantinople. Later sold to British Government for service in Black Sea, supporting the British forces engaged in the Crimean War. *7.1860:* In Government service at Malta. *3.1867:* Sold to Vincenza Gollcher, Malta. *10.1871:* Broken up.

m.v. CALYPSO G (1950-1951), wood twin-screw motor vessel
O.N. 191018. 294gt, 235nt, 130 x 25 x 7 feet
Oil engines (2), each 8-cyl, General Motors Corporation, Cleveland, Ohio.

20.8.1942: Completed by Ballard Marine Railway, Seattle for U.S. Government for lease-lend to Royal Navy as BYMS 26, having been launched on *21.3.1942. 28.2.1943:* Sailed from Seattle as part of No 153 Minesweeping Flotilla for Gibraltar via San Francisco and Freetown. *8.1943:* Based at Malta. *1944:* Renumbered BYMS 2026 and based at Taranto/Naples. *7.1946:* De-commissioned and laid up at Malta. *1.8.1947:* Handed back to U.S. Navy. *5.1949:* Acquired by Joseph Gasan, Malta and converted for commercial service. *7.3.1950:* Renamed CALYPSO G and commenced ferry service. *1.1951:* Sold to Compagnie Oceanographique Francaise, Nice, refitted as an undersea research vessel, and renamed CALYPSO. Still in service.

m.v. CALYPSO LAND — see under PRINS HENDRIK.

m.v. COMINOLAND — see under MINOR EAGLE.

s.s. CONCETTA (1895-1897), wooden launch
O.N. 87616. 34gt, 24nt, 70 x 15 x 8 feet
Compound, 25hp

4.1884: Completed by Pasquale Grech, Malta for his own account. *1885:* Sold to Societa di Pontoni e Lancie, Malta. *26.10.1945:* Officially reported as lost by enemy action, but probably actually lost during 1941/2.

m.v. CYGNET (1947 only), twin-screw wooden motor launch
O.N. 155996. 38gt, 10nt, 56 x 13 x 5 feet
Oil engines (2), 100bhp, Perkins.

6.1934: Completed by J & G. Caruana, Malta for A.C. Torregiani, Malta. *9.1942:* Sold to M. Xuerab, Malta, name unchanged. *6.1947:* Sold to J. Schembri, Malta, name unchanged. *12.1948:* Sold to S.L. Mizzi, Malta, name unchanged. *8.1959:* Sold to Swiss subject — no further record.

s.s. DOLLY (1904-1909), steel screw tug
O.N. 109334. 129gt, 88nt, 93 x 18 x 11 feet
Compound, 32hp, E. Cravero & Co, Genoa.

1891: Completed by Cravero & Co, Genoa for G. Queriolo, Genoa as NUOVO P QUERIOLO. *2.1904:* Sold to S. Mizzi, Malta and renamed DOLLY. *3.1910:* Sold to Impresa P Cacciari, Ancona and renamed FILIPPO. *1927:* Deleted from Lloyd's Register - presumed broken up.

p.s. DRAGON (1856- ?), iron paddle tug
O.N. 22575. 93gt, 13nt, 85 x 17 x 8 feet
Engine 40hp

5.1855: Completed by Palmer Bros & Co, Jarrow (Tyne) for own account and sailed to Mediterranean, probably being stationed at Malta. *11.1860:* Sold to Government for service at Malta. *1868:* Sold to G. Brandenburg, Malta. *1871:* Broken up.

m.v. DUKE OF GLOUCESTER (1932-1939), twin-screw wooden yacht
O.N. 155991. 61gt, 31nt, 68 x 16 x 7 feet
Oil engines (2), each 4-cyl, 90bhp, Parsons Motor Co, Southampton.

6.1932: Completed by Bernard Zammit, Malta for his own account. *8.1939:* Time chartered by Royal Navy as an examination vessel. *2.1940:* Returned to owner. *1.1951:* Broken up at Malta.

DUKE OF GLOUCESTER at Mgarr Pier

s.s. EMILY P (1948 only) wooden screw launch
O.N. 123514. 36gt. 16nt. 61 x 16 x 7 feet
Compound. 20hp. Shanks & Sons Ltd. London

1914: Completed by Lorenzo Gatt. Malta for National Steam Ferry Co. Malta. *1948:* On charter to J. Gasan. Malta for Gozo ferry service for the months of January and February. *11.1960:* Broken up.

s.s. FRANCO (1937-1948), iron screw steamer
O.N. 98755. 153gt, 53nt, 102 x 21 x 11 feet
Compound, 42hp, Muir & Houston, Glasgow

8.1891: Completed by Mackie & Thompson, Glasgow for Kingston Steam Trawler Co Ltd, Hull as PEARL. *7.1912:* Sold to Joseph Constant, London. *8.1912:* Sold to C. Napoli, Catania and renamed SAN FRANCESCO DI PAOLA. *1920:* Sold to Ang. Rallo, Civitavecchia and renamed SELINUTE. *1933:* Sold to Francesco Narissi di Mario, Catania and renamed NEREO. *1935:* Sold to Luigi Saitta & Giacomo, Catania and renamed SALVI. *10.1935:* Sold to Albert Borg, Malta, converted to general cargo, and renamed FRANCO. *12.1939:* Sold to Michale Vella, Malta. *5.1943:* Sold to Gozo Mail Co Ltd, Malta. *4.1948:* Sold to J. Bezzina & Sons, Malta. *8.1948:* Broken up in Italy.

m.v. GHAWDEX (1979-), twin-screw motor ferry
O.N. 0130 (Malta). 2,301gt, 1,043nt, 264 x 53 x 25 feet.
Oil engines (4), each 9-cyl, 5,240bhp, Masch. Augsburg-Nurnberg, Augsburg

1962: Completed by Adler Werft G.m.b.H., Bremen for Juelsminde-Kalundborg Linien A/S, Juelsminde as KALLE. *1971:* Sold to A/S D/S Bornholm af 1861, Ronne and renamed ROTNA. *1.1979:* Acquired by Gozo Channel Co Ltd, and renamed GHAWDEX. Still in service.

GHAWDEX *(Michael Grima)*

s.s. GLENEAGLES (1885-1914), iron screw steamer
O.N. 88864. 207gt, 86nt, 136 x 23 x 11 feet
Compound, 72hp, Hall, Russell & Co, Aberdeen

11.1884: Launched by Hall, Russell & Co, Aberdeen for J. Fleming, Aberdeen. *2.1885:* Sold to O.F. Gollcher & Sons, Malta. *13.6.1885:* Commenced sailings between Malta and Gozo. *1914:* Requisitioned by Royal Navy as an examination vessel. *1918:* Returned to her owners. *4.1919:* Sold to Cassar & Manara, Malta. *29.10.1920:* Sunk at anchor while at Port Said after being struck by Italian s.s. CADMEA. *1922:* Raised and sold to Awaragi Akel & Ragi, Alexandria and renamed MISSIR. *1923:* Sold to P. Abrizi, Alexandretta an renamed ALEXANDRETTA. *1924:* Sold to A.C. Abramudis (M.P. Salvago, manager), Alexandria and renamed PANDY. *1925:* Sold to Youssef & Abdel Kader, Alexandria and renamed ABDEL KADER. *4.3.1933:* Wrecked at Alexandretta.

GLENEAGLES as a wartime examination vessel — 1917

s.s. GOLLY (1923-1937), steel screw steamer
O.N. 152046. 244gt, 82nt, 118 x 22 x 13 feet
Triple expansion, 52hp, Kawasaki Dockyard Co Ltd, Kobe.

1912: Completed by Kawasaki Dockyard Co Ltd, Kobe for Fukuhaku Yenyo Gyogyo K.K., Fukuhaku as FUKUHAKU MARU NO 5. *1916:* Sold to Italian Government for naval service. *2.1917:* Commissioned as Patrol Vessel G 27. *5.1921:* Sold to Salento Soc. Anon. Co-operaitiva di Nav., Taranto and renamed ANDREA BAFILE. *3.1923:* Acquired by Malta S.S. Co Ltd, Malta and renamed GOLLY. *15.8.1932:* Ran ashore near Mgarr but later refloated. *3.1937:* Sold to Ahmed Mohamed Saleh el Faham, Alexandria and renamed DAISY. *1.4.1939:* Foundered in position 33.00N x 34.30E, while on passage from Limassol to Alexandria with general cargo.

GOLLY aground on Comino — August, 1932

HANINI in Grand Harbour — 1976

m.v HANINI (1937-1956), twin-screw steel motor yacht
O.N. 148775. 90gt, 48nt, 86 x 15 x 9 feet
Oil engines (2), each 6-cyl, Atlantic, Wishaw

1926: Completed by George Brown & Co, Greenock for Sir Richard A. Cooper, Bart., London as ALICE. *1933:* Sold to Teodoro Morisoni, Naples. *1937:* Sold to Joseph Gasan, Malta and renamed HANINI. *12.1944:* Sold to Emmanuel Magro, of Victoria, Gozo. *6.1964:* Sold to J.E. Caruana, Malta (for harbour cruises). *4.1974:* Sold to Ghandom Mustafa, Syria and taken in hand for repairs. *11.1978:* Laid-up in Marsa Creek, Grand Harbour. *2.1980:* Sold by auction on the authority of the Director of Ports to meet outstanding port dues, but new owner refused to take delivery because of hull condition.

IMPERIAL EAGLE entering Grand Harbour *(Michael Cassar)*

m.v. IMPERIAL EAGLE (1958-), steel twin-screw motor vessel
O.N. 145671. 257gt, 144nt, 145 x 26 x 7 feet
Oil engines, (2) each 6-cyl, Crossley Bros Ltd, Manchester.

6.1938: Completed by J. Crown & Sons Ltd, Sunderland for Thomas Round & Sons, Scarborough as NEW ROYAL LADY. *3.1940:* Requisitioned by Royal Navy for transport duties. *1.1942:* Purchased by MOWT (Fraser & White, managers) for transport duties. *9.1944:* Attached to U.S. Navy. *2.1945:* Transferred to port defence duties. *1.1946:* Resold to original owners. *4.1947:* Sold to John Hall, Kirkcaldy for service on Firth of Forth, and renamed ROYAL LADY. *11.1947:* Sold to General Steam Navigation Co Ltd, London for Thames dock cruises, and renamed CRESTED EAGLE. *11.1957:* Sold to Magro Bros, Malta and towed out to Malta from Thames. *2.6.1958:* After modification to carry cars, renamed IMPERIAL EAGLE and commenced sailings to Gozo. *20.5.1968:* Laid-up in Marsa Creek to await disposal. *8.1972:* Resumed sailing to Gozo but from Grand Harbour. Now owned by Mrs L. Magro, widow of last surviving brother. *1978:* Sold to Pisani Bros, of Victoria, Gozo. Still in service.

s.t. IS-SAJJED (1939-1942) — no details available.

JYLLAND as a cruise ship 1979 *(Michael Grima)*

m.v. JYLLAND (1967-1978), steel twin-screw motor vessel
O.N. 332318. 824gt, 283nt, 188 x 33 x 9 feet
Oil engines (2), each 12-cyl, General Motors Corporation, La Grange (USA).

15.5.1943: Completed by Pullman Car Standard Manufacturing Co, Chicago for U.S. Navy as Submarine Chaser (Escort) PCE 828, having been launched on *17.11.1942. 31.7.1943:* Transferred to Royal Navy as Patrol Vessel and renamed HMS KILBRIDE. *10.12.1946:* Handed back to U.S. Navy. *2.1948:* Sold to A/S Kristiansands Dampskibsselskap, Kristiansand and converted to car ferry by Stord Vaerft, Moss. *1949:* Renamed JYLLAND and placed on ferry service between Kristiansand and Hirtshals (Denmark), with capacity for 32 cars and 650 passengers. *12.1967:* Sold to E. Zammit & Sons, Malta for £100,000. *19.1.1968:* Sailed from Kristiansand for Malta, via Tyne (21/1), and Plymouth (24/1). *1.2.1968:* Arrived Grand Harbour. *20.5.1968:* Commenced ferry sailings between Mgarr and Marfa. *1973/4:* During summer months, operated a service between Malta and Syracuse. *1978:* Withdrawn from ferry services. *1979:* Commenced operating island cruises (summer only). Still in service.

m.v. JYLLAND II — see under MINOR EAGLE

s.s. KING OF ENGLAND (1933-1944), steel screw steamer
O.N. 155992. 194gt, 96nt, 116 x 21 x 9 feet
Triple expansion, 41hp, Bow, McLachlan & Co, Paisley.

30.9.1932: Launched by Bow, McLachlan & Co, Paisley as Royal Navy tank vessel HELPFUL. *18.11.1933:* Acquired by Bernard Zammit, Malta, converted for commercial service and renamed KING OF ENGLAND. *5.1942:* Requisitioned by Royal Navy as a salvage vessel. *7.1942:* Returned to her owners. *4.1944:* Sold to Galzamhil Co Ltd, Malta. *3.1951:* Sold to Mario Farrugia, Malta. *4.1951:* Broken up in Italy.

s.s. LADY DOWNSHIRE (1886-1901), iron screw steamer
O.N. 63956. 254gt, 139nt, 140 x 21 x 10 feet
Compound, 50hp, Walker Henderson & Co, Glasgow

10.1873: Launched by Macfadyen & Co, Port Glasgow for East Downshire S.S. Co. Belfast. *3.1886:* Acquired by O.F. Gollcher & Sons, Malta. *8.1901:* Sold to E. Malucci, Ancona and renamed ADRIATICO. *18.12.1901:* Wrecked at Brioni, while on passage from Catania to Trieste with wine and vegatables.

s.s. LADY STRICKLAND (1930-1933), twin-screw steel launch
O.N. 152058. 59gt, 16nt, 77 x 17 x 9 feet
Compound, 11hp, Cox & Co, Falmouth

1887: Completed by Cox & Co, Falmouth for War Department as SIR JOHN JONES. *11.1906:* Tranferred to Royal Navy and renamed PELICAN. *14.10.1916:* Renamed PETULANT. *23.5.1927:* Acquired by Bernardo Zammit, Malta, converted for commercial service, and renamed LADY STRICKLAND. *1.1951:* Sold to Royal Navy, who after removing her boiler for use in the Dockyard, Malta, dismantled her hull.

LORD STRICKLAND outward bound for Syracuse —1949

m.v. LORD STRICKLAND (1947 only), wooden twin-screw motor vessel
O.N. 175809. 302gt, 200nt, 129 x 25 x 9 feet
Oil engines (2), each 8-cyl, General Motors Corporation, Cleveland, Ohio.

7.9.1942: Completed by Greenpoint Basin & Construction Co, Greenpoint, NY for U.S. Navy as minesweeper 187, having been launched on *27.6.1942. 12.3.1943:* Transferred to Royal Navy and renumbered BYMS 2187. *10.7.1947:* Handed back to U.S. Navy. *10.1947:* Sold to Anglia Shipping Co Ltd, Malta, converted for commercial service, and renamed LORD STRICKLAND. *5.12.1947:* Chartered to J. Gasan, Malta for one month to operate Mgarr-Marfa ferry. *1.1948:* Commenced sailing between Malta and Syracuse. *7.1952:* Sold to Compagnie de Nav. Mixte Societe Cooperative, Puerto Limon, name unchanged. *1955:* Deleted from Lloyd's Register — no further record.

m.v. MAID OF PINTO (1951 only), wooden motor fishing vessel
O.N. 191772. 203gt, 110nt, 91 x 22 x 8 feet
Oil engine, 4-cyl, Crossley Bros Ltd, Manchester.

1944: Completed by Frank Curtis Ltd, Par (Cornwall) for Royal Navy as MFV 1517. *17.1.1950:* Acquired by Mediterranean Shipbreaking & Salvage Co Ltd (Maltese flag) and renamed MAID OF PINTO. *1.1954:* Sold to D.C. Maxwell (British flag). *11.1954:* Sold to unknown French owners, and sailed to New Caledonia — no further record.

aux.s.v. MARIE GORGETTE - no details available

MELITA LAND as **DORDRECHT** prior to her rebuild in 1955 *(J.J. Steketee)*

m.v. MELITA LAND (1972-), steel double-ended screw ferry
O.N. 0047. (Malta) ?gt, ?nt, 133 x 34 x 15 feet; lengthened 1955 - work carried out by N.V. Terneuzensche Scheepsbouw Maatschappij, being rebuilt as a ro-ro ferry, with additional side loading facilities, now 231 x 44 x 15 feet, 1,435gt, 1,051nt
Triple expansion, 550ihp, Penn en Bauduin Machinefabriek LJzergietery & Constructiewerkplaats, Dordrecht; converted to m.v. 1956, oil engines (4) driving 4 electric motors, 610bhp, each pair geared to two shafts, each motor 8-cyl, Lister-Blackstone Diesels Ltd, Dursley (UK).

5.1933: Completed by N.V. Meyer & Co's Scheepsbouw-Maatschappij, Zaltbommel for the Dutch Government (Department of Waterways) as DORDRECHT, for service across the Hollandsch Diep at Moerdijk — capacity 30 cars and 1000 passengers. *1936:* Chartered to Provinciale Stoombootdiensten in Zeeland, Middelburg for service across Westerschelde (Flushing — Breskins), when bridge replaced ferry service at Moerdijk. *5.1955:* On lengthening, capacity 80 cars and 600 passengers. *9.1956:* Converted to m.v. by N.V. Koninklijke Maatschappij "De Schelde", Flushing. *1.1972:* Sold to A.C. Slooten Handelsonderneming & Bergingbedrijf, Wormer. *1.1973:* Acquired by E. Zammit & Sons, Malta and dry docked in Holland. *2.1974:* Renamed MELITA LAND and departed for Malta. *15.2.1974:* Arrived at Bilbao in tow of Dutch tug ENGELAND, after breaking down in Bay of Biscay. *19.2.1974:* Sailed from Bilbao in tow for Gibraltar. *25.2.1974:* Arrived at Gibraltar, where spares had arrived from UK, and sailed under own power 4 days later. *5.3.1974:* Arrived Grand Harbour. *16.6.1974:* Commenced summer sailings on Marfa service (laid up during winters). *2.1980:* Sold to Gozo Channel Co Ltd, name unchanged. *6.1980:* Resumed sailings Gozo — Cirkewwa. Still in service.

MELITA LAND off Paradise Bay Pier *(G.H. Somner)*

MGARR leaving Mgarr *(Michael Grima)*

m.v. MGARR (1980-   ), twin-screw motor ferry
O.N. 0503 (Malta). 728gt, 302nt, 163 x 35 x 10 feet
Oil engines (2), each 6-cyl, 1,320bhp, A/B Jonkopings Motorfabrik, Jonkoping, Sweden

1967: Completed by Aalborg Vaerft A/S, Aalborg, Denmark for Svenska R/A Oresund, Malmo as SALTHOLM. *12.1979:* Acquired by Gozo Channel Co Ltd. *3.1980:* Renamed MGARR. Still in service.

COMINOLAND entering Grand Harbour *(Michael Cassar)*

m.v. MINOR EAGLE/COMINOLAND/JYLLAND II (1968-1979), steel twin-screw motor vessel
O.N. 332329. 295gt. 150nt. 113 x 27 x 12 feet
Oil engines (2). each 6-cyl. Ruston & Hornsby Ltd. Lincoln — new engines fitted 1976. General Motors Corporation (USA).

7.2.1942: Completed by Philip & Son Ltd. Dartmouth for Royal Navy as H.M. coastal minelayer M 6 (later MINER 6). having been launched on *22.4.1941*. *10.1966:* Acquired by E. Zammit & Sons, Malta. *1968:* Converted for commercial service. and renamed MINOR EAGLE. *1976:* Renamed COMINOLAND. *7.1980:* Renamed JYLLAND II. *1980/81:* Laid-up at Msida (except for a few weeks).

m.v. NANRIDI (1947 only), wooden twin-screw motor vessel
O.N. 175910. 311gt, 222nt, 129 x 25 x 9 feet
Oil engines (2), each 8-cyl, General Motors Corporation, Cleveland Ohio.

1943: Completed by American Car & Foundry Co, Wilmington for US Government for lease-lend to Royal Navy as HM minesweeper BYMS 2031. *1947:* Sold to A. Theuma & P.P. Moore, Malta, converted for commercial service, and renamed NANRIDI. *1.11.1947:* Chartered to J. Gasan, Malta for Marfa ferry. *1.1950:* Sailed to Messina, to be sold to M. Galea, Gibraltar and renamed MONTE CARMELO. Later sailed to Tangier. Subsequently captured off Palermo whilst attempting to smuggle tobacco into Italy. *6.1966:* Italian authorities officially declared the vessel confiscated — no further record.

s.s. PIEMONTE (1897-1901), iron screw steamer
O.N. 105118. 397gt, 244nt, 178 x 24 x 12 feet
Compound, 130hp, Palmer Bros & Co, Newcastle — new engines fitted 1870, compound, 90hp, Westerman Bros, Sestri Ponente.

10.1863: Launched by Palmer Bros & Co, Newcastle for R. Rubbatino, Genoa. *9.1881:* Sold to Nav. Gen. Italiana, Genoa, name unchanged. *1896:* Sold to G. Messina, Genoa, name unchanged. *12.1897:* Acquired by Francesco Pace, Malta, name unchanged. *6.1901:* Sold to Italian owners and renamed SEMPE PIEMONTE. *1902:* Sold to E. Basart, Barcelona and renamed NEPTUNO. *1907:* Broken up.

m.v. PINU (1956-1957), wooden screw motor vessel
O.N. 199202. 235gt, 93nt, 114 x 22 x 8 feet
Oil engine, 500bhp, Mirrlees, Bickerton & Day Ltd, Stockport.

10.6.1942: Completed by F. Curtis, Totnes for Royal Navy as HM minesweeper MMS 172. *1946/7:* Lent to Italian Navy and renumbered DR 214. *1948:* Royal Navy renumbered her MMS 1672. *7.1956:* Acquired by Joseph Gasan, Malta, converted for commercial service, and renamed PINU. *12.1957:* Sold to Greek owners — no further record.

s.s. PRINCESS MELITA (1893-1924), steel screw steamer
O.N. 101546. 120gt, 51nt, 113 x 18 x 8 feet
Compound, 50hp, J. Scott & Co, Kinghorn.

1893: Completed by J. Scott & Co, Kinghorn for G.P. Sammut & Co, Malta. *15.9.1893:* Arrived at Grand Harbour from Burntisland, Fife. *10.1913:* Gustaf Gollcher (of O.F. Gollcher & Sons) became managing owner. *2.1916:* Sold to Colonel Alexander Mattei, Malta. *9.1923:* Passed to Mrs C. Mattei, Malta. *1924:* Broken up.

CALYPSO LAND approaching Marfa Pier *(G.H. Somner)*

m.v. PRINS HENDRIK/CALYPSO LAND (1969-1978), steel double-ended screw ferry
O.N. 0068 (Malta). 518gt, 34nt, 165 x 41 x 13 feet — lengthened 1941 to 192 feet, 672gt, 190nt
Oil engine, 6-cyl, driving dynamo for 2 electric motors, 550hp each, Schelde-Sulzer, Flushing — new engine fitted 1949 (made 1932). oil engine, 8-cyl, new motors now 850hp, Werkspoor-Sulzer, Amsterdam.

20.6.1932: Launched by N.V. Koninklijke Maatschappij "De Schelde", Flushing for Provinciale Stoombootdiensten in Zeeland, Middelburg for service across Westerschelde (Flushing — Breskins) — capacity for 25 cars and 750 passengers. *20.9.1932:* Commenced service. *17.5.1940:* Scuttled by Dutch Authorities in Breskins harbour on invasion of Holland by Germany. *19.8.1940:* Raised and towed to builders yard for repairs, and replacement of superstructure removed during salvage operations. *30.8.1941:* Taken in hand for lengthening in drydock. *11.2.1942:* Lengthening completed and vessel laid-up. *10.1944:* Scuttled by German forces in harbour mouth at Flushing on approach of Allied Armies into Holland. *10.6.1947:* Raised and returned to builders for repairs. *10.12.1949:* Returned to service — capacity now 35 cars and 1300 passengers. *1968:* Sold to E. Zammit & Sons, Malta. *28.3.1969:* Sailed from Flushing in tow of tug FAIRPLAY XI. *5.4.1969:* Passed Gibraltar. *10.4.1969:* Arrived in Grand Harbour. *4.1969:* Commenced on Marfa ferry sailings. *1970:* Renamed CALYPSO LAND. *1978:* Withdrawn from ferry service. *1979/81:* Employed carrying building supplies to Comino when not laid-up.

m.v. QUEEN OF PEACE (1956-1970), wooden screw motor vessel
O.N. 199176. 214gt, 93nt, 114 x 22 x 8 feet
Oil engine, 390bhp, Harland & Wolff Ltd, Belfast.

31.3.1942: Completed by Cory Clapson & Sons, Barton-on-Humber for Royal Navy as HM minesweeper MMS 135. *1946/7:* Lent to Italian Navy and renumbered DR 212. *1948:* Royal Navy renumbered her MMS 1635. *9.1955:* Acquired by Magro Bros, Gozo, converted for commercial use, and renamed QUEEN OF PEACE. *1.9.1970:* Laid up in Marsa Creek, Grand Harbour. *9.1972:* Sold to E. Trevisan, Malta. *1975:* Sold to J.P. Ehrnann (French). *10.1975:* After docking, and whilst on trials, ran aground off Malta and severely damaged her stern. *11.1976:* Repairs completed but again laid up in Marsa Creek. *25.11.1977:* While sailing under Mali flag, foundered in heavy seas in Gulf of Sirte, while on passage from Reggio Calabria to Benghai, with loss of 3 crew (4 saved).

QUEEN OF PEACE in Grand Harbour *(Viktor Wickman)*

ROYAL LADY at Mgarr

m.v. ROYAL LADY (1937-1942), steel twin-screw motor vessel
O.N. 145668. 195gt, 129nt, 127 x 24 x 8 feet
Oil engines (2), each 10-cyl, Crossley Bros Ltd, Stockport.

7.1934: Completed by John Crown & Sons Ltd, Sunderland for Thomas Round, Scarborough as first off-shore motor excursion vessel in UK. *9.1937:* Sold to Orazio Mizzi, Malta. *1.11.1937:* Commenced sailings between Mgarr and Marfa. *3.1938:* Transferred to Gozo Mail Co Ltd, (Gatt & Grech, managers) Malta. *8.1939:* Time chartered by Royal Navy as examination vessel. *2.1940:* Requisitioned by Royal Navy for same duties. *8.1940:* Returned to owners for Gozo service. *4.5.1942:* Machine gunned by German aircraft whilst lying at Mgarr, 2 crew killed. *7.5.1942:* Bombed and sunk whilst lying at Mgarr. *1945:* Wreckage dispersed.

aux.s.v. SAN BERT (1957-58) — no details available.

s.s. SIR FILIPPO SCEBERRAS/WEMBLEY (1922-1934), iron screw steamer
O.N. 152045. 154gt, 66nt, 105 x 21 x 10 feet
Triple expansion, 49hp, C.D. Holmes & Co Ltd, Hull.

1892: Completed by Cook, Welton, & Gemmell Ltd, Hull for C. Hellyer & Co, Hull as trawler BROXHOLME (ON 99587). *3.1906:* Sold to R. de la Valle, (Spanish flag) and renamed BOHEMI. *2.1916:* Sold to Italian Government for service as a minesweeper and renamed STROMBOLI. *12.1919:* Sold to Maltese Fishing Co (Italian flag) and renamed NAUTILUS. *1922:* Sold to F.S. Mizzi, Malta and renamed SIR FILIPPO SCEBERRAS. *1.1923:* Owners became F.A. Mizzi, G. Busutil, R. College & others, Malta. *2.1924:* Transferred to Malta S.S. Co, Malta and renamed WEMBLEY. *11.1934:* Sold to Guiseppe Papa, Syracuse and renamed CARMELO PAPA. *1937:* Sold to Luigi Savoia, Palermo, and later to Fratelli Savaca, Palermo — renamed FORTUNATO. *1938:* Broken up.

(Note — Vessel issued with another official number in 1922 due to a clerical error when she reverted to the British flag. Original O.N. was 99587)

s.s. SOUTH WESTERN (1859 only), iron screw steamer
O.N. 20893. 210gt, 127nt, 139 x 20 x 10 feet
2-cyl, 45hp, Blackwood & Gordon, Paisley — new engine 1872, compound, 2-cyl, 40hp, Blair & Co Ltd, Stockton.

1858: Completed by Blackwood & Gordon, Paisley for George Madder & B. Bremner, Cork. *10.1858:* Sold to T. Mackie & others, Dublin. *8.1859:* Ownership reverted to G. Madder, with instructions to sell vessel within 6 months for not less than £4,400. *10.1859:* Sold at Malta to foreign owners, and renamed MEULADIA. *9.1868:* Sold to G.L Tod, Malta in a damaged condition, renamed DIDO and sailed to UK. *10.1868:* Sold to Thomas Henderson (of Anchor Line), Glasgow. *6.1871:* Owner now John Henderson, Glasgow. *7.1871:* Sold to James Luke, Dundee. *6.1872:* Sold to Peter Barr & A. Fawcett, Glasgow. *5.1873:* Sold to London & Edinburgh Shipping Co Ltd, Leith. *6.1880:* Sold to R. Blagdon, London as agents for Brazilian owners, and sailed out to Maranhao, Brazil. *11.9.1880:* Stranded off Viscu while on passage from Para to Parnaiba and Maranhao. Later refloated and taken to Maranhao. *25.9.1880:* Taken in tow for Demerara by French s.s. JEUNE AMIRAL where repairs to stern post to be carried out — no further record after that date.

p.s. SOVEREIGN (1856- ?) — no details available.

ROSINA M in Grand Harbour *(Vicktor Wickman)*

s.s. SUPPLY (1948-1949), twin-screw steamer/motor vessel
O.N. 191009. 228gt, 153nt, 115 x 21 x 10 feet
Compound, 300hp, Cox & Co (Engineers) Ltd, Falmouth — oil engine fitted 1949, 6-cyl, Ansaldo S.A., Genoa.

1910: Completed by Cox & Co (Engineers) Ltd, Falmouth for the Royal Navy as waterboat SUPPLY. *10.1947:* Sold to Coleiro Navigation Co Ltd, Malta and converted for the carriage of wine from Gozo. *3.1948:* Chartered by J. Gasan, Malta to operate Mgarr — Marfa sailings. *11.1949:* Converted to motor vessel and renamed ROSINA M. *11.1973:* Broken up in Italy after having been laid up for some years.

s.s. WEMBLEY — see under SIR FILIPPO SCEBERRAS

Mgarr Harbour — 1951
(**BANCINU** approaching pier with **HANINI** tied-up alongside.) *(Michael Grima)*

Mgarr Harbour with its new breakwater — 1976
(**MELITA LAND** entering harbour, **COMINOLAND** and **IMPERIAL EAGLE** lying alongside quay, and **JYLLAND** at her summer lying-up berth.) *(Micheal Grima)*